Acknowledgements

Dedicated to my lovely wife, Carolyn, who has stuck by me and encouraged me in any endeavor I have attempted, in our 28 years of marriage. My sister-in-law, Ethel McGaw, who printed the manuscript for every book I've written and copyrighted, including *Borum's Delight in Poetry*, and *The Common Touch*, Thanks to all my friends who were the source of some of my material.

Life's *Candid* Treasure Chest
TXu 2-023-645
All Rights Reserved

No portion of this publication may be reproduced, stored in any electronic system or transmitted in any form by any means, electronic, mechanical, photocopy, recording, or otherwise, without written permission from the author. Brief quotations may be used in literary reviews. Unless otherwise indicated, all scripture quotations are taken from the King James Version of the Bible.

By William Borum, Jr.
All Rights Reserved
Library of Congress
TXu 2-023-645
March 2016
ISBN: 978-0-9975037-4-6

This is a work of fiction. Names, characters, businesses, places, events and incidents are either the products of the author's imagination or used in a fictitious manner. Any resemblance to actual persons, living or dead, or actual events is purely coincidental.

Preface

In 1991, the World of Poetry, over 1.7 million poets strong (worldwide) presented William an award merit certificate for the poem "A Child's Thoughts". He has received a Golden Poet trophy for the poem "Zeal Where Art Thou" (Changed to 'Lamentation'), and is listed as one of the best new poets of 1988 by the American Poetry Association.

William Borum, affectionately known to his friends as 'Zeke', decided one day, during a spell of illness to write about his life in poetry, prose, and short stories. He was not sure he could write another poem or anything after his first poem, but through perseverance and inspiration, he began writing poem after poem. Then he fell into a dry spell, for lack of a better word, 'the mind went blank'. he would began again. Anyone going through similar struggles and need understanding of how to cope when life takes a turn against you, and If you are determined to make a success after a two year layoff. These writings are intended to help someone like himself who did not live a good family life as a child. Now a mature man in his seventies he looks back remembering his roots and thanking God that the experience made him a better person. He is now happily married and has struggled and sacrificed his life to the Lord Jesus Christ. He is now a leader in the Church of God In Christ. All of his writings point back to his childhood which he has never regretted. These writings are geared to help you with problems in your life. The poet desires each child a debut, a time to express their individuality and significance.

When any of his children appear neglected, the poet is troubled until his hard labor or inspiration brings the child a place of respectability. Let the dreamer's dream and help mold some positive realities that meet the people's need. Let the realist enlighten you about life's crude awakening. William's desire is that these writings will touch someone's life in a positive and meaningful way. He knows that experiences in life take on no greater significance than when it is shared with others as lessons learned.

Writings from Life's *Candid* Treasure Chest |

Table of Content

Title	Page
Dad Said Nothing	1
The Promise	3
The Calling	4
Careers	6
Brainwashed to Survive	7
The Put Down	8
The Token	9
Ebony/Ivory	10
Wise Guy	11
Exit at Death's Door	12
Impropriety	14
Disquieted Soul	17
Manhood/Womanhood	19
Nature's Retreat	23
The Pursuit of Happiness	25
Metamorphosis	27
To Robyn with Love	30
The Elusive Vein	32
Fruit of Compassion	34
Lamentation	38

Sin Scarred	40
Echoes in the Night	42
Mirrored	48
Flesh and Blood	49
The Living Zombie	51
Gang Busters	54
At a Glance	56
Despairing Posterity	65
May the Best Man Win	65
No More Biscuits	67
Two Peas In a Pod	70
The Sower Shall Reap	72
Subtle Parsimony	75
Lest We Forget	76
This Thing Called Love	79
Foolish Pride	82
Abode Rodent	85
Party Chit Chat	87

Life' *Candid* Treasure Chest

Dad Said Nothing
(deprived)

His mom worked hard all day, just to keep their heads above water.

His dad was here and there, only God knows where.

One day she told him he could go to college, but dad said nothing.

Could he put his mom through this great sacrifice to fulfill his selfish desire?

Dad said nothing.

If he wanted to he could go, she reminded him,

but dad said nothing.
How wonderful it would be to earn a degree, he thought...
I wonder how dad feels about it.
But dad said nothing.

He decided not to go, ... and, dad still said nothing.

The Promise

Shades of yellow, orange and red.
Shade of green, shade of blue,
violet and indigo.
Arched within the glowing,
Beginning somewhere and ending
the same.
The rains have come and pranced
the night away, leaving a trail of
colors, to remember the story of the
promise.
Contrary to the awe stricken
creatures, fabled tale of a pot of
gold, should you find its earthly
resting place. Those who are wise in
the knowledge thereof knows that
this was in fact a new beginning.
The treasured ... Promise.

The Calling

All he had learned from the Bible would eventually determine his destiny. From his understanding of life's options, he made his choice. He took the road where sin could not claim his immortal soul. The road would be narrow, the way tedious, but he knew to be empowered by the Holy Spirit would assure an undeniable victory. His faith had taught him that life at times, would appear as an unquestionable defeat.

Did he possess the whole amour? ... Was he ready or over zealous? Knowing that faith without works is dead, he took up his cross and began the journey.

———————

Careers

(two black men conversing about their
white guidance teacher)

Hey man, you take the
Guidance test?
...sure did.
How'd you make out?
Well man, he told me
I was only fit for manual labor.
That's strange man??!!...
What'cha talkin about?
That's what he told me too.

Brainwashed to Survive

Now son,
Listen to your Mama.
When you go to your job,
You do what you're told to do.
Mind your own business,
Don't give your boss no trouble.
Don't cause no flack
Be thankful you got a job.

The Put Down

Sit'n here thinking,
The Lord sho'dun blessed us.
Now take Mary,
She dun gone to school
to become a real estate agent.
Howard runs the car rental business,
David is bout to git his master's degree...
And you son,...when are you gonna git
a better job?

———————

The Token

Hey Bud! Got a diploma?
"Yes"
The whites you work with
Ain't got no diplomas
But, hey man, I ain't jokin'
You can get the job now
Its been mandated
They need a token

———————

Ebony/Ivory

I don't understand
Why some folks don't like,...you people,
Why,...I was raised up with,...you people
Played in the back yard,
With...you people.
Went to school with,...you coloreds
I've never been prejudice against,...you people.

Wise Guy

Hey Zeke!
I wonder who told me
You had a football head?

Hey Fitzgerald!
The same one that told me,
You had a basketball head.

Exit at Death's Door

Suspicion,... reality strikes
Like a thief in the night.
Melancholy a constant
companion.
Loneliness unfinished goals,
Confusion, depression,... the
question "why?" "How?"
A familiar face, nevertheless a
stranger.
The inevitable is making its
debut.
Must set my house in order
The computer access, its data
banks.

Projections flash upon the
screen.
The invisible eye scanning the
yesteryears.
Within this dispirited soul,... joy,
sorrow,
The hope for tomorrows have
all wound down,
To ebbing cherished moments,
Priorities unchallenged,
To forgive,... to be forgiven,
prerequisites before the expired
transformation,
Exit.

Impropriety
(she was acting out of insecurity)

An incident occurred the other day,
She hesitated to confront him for fear,
He might uncover that which
She did not want him to know,
It was to remain her secret.
Anger, hurt feelings pursued,
A clearly devised plot took shape,
She would ignore his feelings,
Use his friend against him.
She had to know,

Could she make him jealous?
Feelings he had aroused in her.
She would confide in his friend,
not him.
Did the close friendship she
shared with him matter?
What would be his reaction?
Could she use this approach

Without raising suspicion.
He approached her in a public
place,
He wanted to know why,
She confided in his friend but
not him.

She looked in his eyes,
And knew, he was hurting
Within she was rejoicing,
But her lips and eyes said, I'm sorry.
She wondered if he suspected.

Disquieted Soul

Skin and bones poured out upon,
Cotton, coils, wood and cloth.
Nature's hot breath drifting through,
The window screens.
The whispering trees
Hum a redundant tune.
While images reflect
Upon the mirror of time.
His soul entertains no single emotion
The propeller driven breeze,
Giving temporary comfort

Shall take its rest,
Through the dormant seasons.
But ghosts of the past know no season.
Whenever the trigger is pulled.
They make their debut.
When the bones of this soul have gone dry,
While piled in a wooden box below,
With the earth pressing to caress them,
Some ghosts will linger to taunt
And perhaps destroy the lives of others.
But there is an answer to every problem,... Try Jesus.

Manhood/Womanhood

How well did he remember
Wondering what the future would hold,
While his sheltered world sustained him
His dreams were vivid and bold.
His mind was unbridled, free,
He could be whatever he was purposed to be.
The clock ticked away the hours
The years came and were lost forever,
Like the elusive April showers.

His mind endowed with the curse of his generation
He began his journey into manhood
With a weaker but wiser nation.
Responsibility was a word he knew
And thought he handled it well,
But responsibility and accountability
Became a formidable task
Seemed harder to face each day.
That's when he awakened to the realization... To be a man is more than the coming of age,

One must be willing to face
life's many challenges...And see
them through to victorious
beginnings.
He learned that faith could
keep you strong in your weakest
hour,
Dark clouds bring showers of
despair
But time brings about a change
He became a man not for
reaching the age of twenty one.
But for the battles he was
courageously fighting,
And winning in his life's
struggles,

To become master of his humble existence.

———————

Nature's Retreat

How do the lines appear?
All in their proper place.

Who them all can count?
Who is knowledgeable to really understand?

Too soon? ...not a second
Too late? ...not a minute

They appear displaying times
Creativity, who void of conscience

Enhance the wrinkled impressions
Common to the regressing shelter
Housing the indwelling spirit.

Through those energetic,
joyous,
tumultuous years ever,

Sustaining its authority,
Against mortal eternity.

All creatures on the journey
Back from whence we come.

The Pursuit of Happiness

Life is like a lawn of grass.
We plant grass seeds;
The better the blend, the
better the grass.
Crab grass is not wanted.
We don't have to plant it.
It grows all by it self.
Those who desire the best lawn
Are continuously pulling out
the crabgrass before it spreads,
And choke out the good grass,
Nutritious soil is subject to
both.

So we are left with a choice.
In this life when we choose to plant the best of seeds,
With such a loneliness of heart
We do not plant crabgrass: disappointments, sorrow, stress, sickness, —But they grow up together
We find joy, happiness and a fulfilling life,—When we accept this truth.
Then and only then can we be victorious in this battle,
Acknowledging Christ to be the answer to every problem.

Metamorphosis

The cocoon is broken.
No longer does the larva crawl
...behold the butterfly!

The psychological, emotional,
and spiritual
State of being has victoriously
travailed,

Through this arduous
transformation
...of mind and spirit.

Now Lord,...please lead me up

where I belong
Knowing your eyes are continually upon me.
I'll flutter my wings against the winds,

Of the provocative challenging moments In my life.
I'll take flight to survey those foreign lands,

Searching from shore to sandy shore
Capturing the elusive questions
Then sifting them to salvage the gold,

Seeking to balance the needs against the desires.

To be sure prayer will provide the answers.
And God's abundance shall not pass me by.

To Robyn with Love

Robyn, dear Robyn
Sowing your seeds of passion,
Only to fall upon stony ground,
While searching for that fertile land
To nurture your most sacred emotions
Where love, caring, commitment
Can flourish freely
Between two souls,
And can grow uninhibited
Despite the despicable tares of
The inherent inhabitants
That strive to choke out

The very existence of a soul mate.
Within this haven (you are searching)
Only death can separate.
After the needs of the flesh have vanished.
Eternity shall have the final say.
Can human love aspire and reach
This pinnacle, of itself ..no.
But when Christ is the center of our lives,
And if in His will dwells as our continual delight
He will supply our every need.

The Elusive Vein
(writers block)

Digging, searching, digging,...
Exploring to find another vein,
We try and try again but to no avail..
Then one day without warning..
Eureka!
We draw from that dormant deposit
Laden with an avalanche of thoughts
Recollections, new ideas flow freely
As though from an eternal force
And like the abundant thunder shower

It is soon spent,
Leaving a residue of
impressions
We continue to dig, but until we are
Certain, the well as gone dry,
We do not move from this place
To start a new.

Fruit of Compassion

Who is this old man?
With the hump upon
his shoulder
Bent with age.

Arms reversed and hands
clasped behind his belly.
The lad was quick to
feel compassion.
He, the old man, seemed
such a lonely, poor humble soul.
Yet he gleaned a youthful
anticipation from the old man's
eyes,

But his consuming compassion blinded his sense of reasoning that lay dormant within. his soul.

He became anxious to recapture the sense of sharing

Sir, ...he addressed the old man. Without hesitation or reservation,... he beckoned, and said,
Come with me, I shall treat you to breakfast this morning - - -
Thank you, the old man replied. After entering the diner which was only a few doors down the street,

The young man sat at the counter and motioned to the old man to sit beside him,
But the old man continued to walk until he was behind the counter.
The young man's eyes grew wide with bewilderment
Which turned to astonishment and embarrassment.
As the old man instructed his workers
To give the young lad whatsoever

He desired to eat
And they responded, yes sir boss.

———————

Lamentation

Out in the cotton field
Every morning by sunrise,
Picking and toting cotton bags,
Through the hot
sweaty
dusty day
They
toiled.
The greater the pickings
The more money to be made.
When pop, realized how well
The family worked together
He decided they would go in
business
For themselves.

Back to the hot sweaty-dusty-task they went.

A new song in his heart,
A new beginning,
But to pops surprise
The young folks worked with diminished fervor,
And left the bags of cotton,
Partially filled out in the open field.

———————————

Sin Scarred

His bones were tired and weary,
His thoughts perplexed and dreary,
His soul cried out to be at peace.
He rambled about like a wounded beast,
He was as dry (his spirit) as the dessert sand.
He needed a touch, a soothing hand
He cried out,... let me stand
In the healing waters of the narrow stream.

To partake of that grand ole scheme
Lord cleanse my untamed tongue
I'm getting ready for redemption,...
...ha-le-llu-jah!

Echoes In The Night

All skate, ladies only, reverse
Couples, trio, waltz and special
Wow! Ain't that something
Through the air the music floats
Smoothly beneath the
peppermint lights
The roar of a thousand wheels
Joined the melodious strains.
Roll on everybody, roll on
Some tall, some short, big, little
and small roll on.
Look see us glide, we ride
So smooth and graceful-
Over this hard wood sea.

Hey! Look over here at me
Watch me go... Oops!
Look at this--
See how easy, one.. Two..
One.. Two.
Mommy! Daddy!
Look at me-e-e
Ouch! I can really skate pretty good,
But I'll fool everybody tonight.
I'll act very casual about my ability.
Next time, I'm gonna show everybody.

Ha!. Gee its kinda lonesome out here.

I don't know anybody.

Daddy! Daddy! I can skate good now!

Ker-plun-k.. I just tripped, that's all.

Whee-e-e this is great fun.

Oops! Sorry

Black, white, red and yellow together.

Who cares, we're having fun -- a common bond.

Gee, look at those two skaters!

Are they for real.. Or out of a story book.

Perhaps Alice-in-wonderland.
Such perfection.
Watch out for the rail!
Whoo-osh.. Boy they're fast.
What!! They can skate better backwards than I can forward.
My..my..my that music can put rhythm in the weariest bones.
Look at that great big skater.. Must be at least two and a half feet tall.
Skate people.. Skate.. Leave all your troubles behind.
Feel them float away in the breeze.
Hey kids, lookout---

there's a pile up.
Oh! Oh! All I want for Christmas is a pair of skates.
Then you could wish me happy bouncing.
I'm a little shaky now, but after a few practice rounds.
I'll be all over the floor... Thump, ..uh..oh I may be in uniform but these civies have nothing on me.
Crunch.. Crunch.. Crunch.. Crunch a bunch of greetos... corn chips.
Smiling faces, see how they smile at me.

Whirl.. Whirl.. Whirl.. You whirly birds.
Roll to the rhythm of the music.
There's a fight! ..a fight!
Where?? In the ladies room.
If you don't shut your big mouth,
I'm gonna put my fist in it.
You and what army?!?
Step aside, here comes an usher.
All right girls! ..break it up..
Right now!

My goodness, he butted in before it got good. Good night.

Mirrored

Whenever you're up speaking son,
Try not to talk so much about your self.
People will interpret that to be bragging.
The one thing I can't tolerate is a braggart.
The father looked at his son,
Son, where did you learn that?
The son looked back with a loving but bewildered smile and said,
I learned it from you dad!

Flesh and Blood

My children are gown but they still live with me. I have two daughters.

JoAnn, would do better but she had bad breaks. Bertha had no luck with her marriage; just married the wrong man. James my son would have done very well but he was enticed by that crack crowd. When my sister Jane comes to visit, all she talks about is her son Tim who became an accountant; her daughter

Kim who models clothes on television, or her daughter Samone who is a buyer. Who wants to hear all those lies. Our mother is sick and Jane would not give her one blanket out of the ten she bought.

She has another daughter, Mary, just recovering from drug addiction. She does not talk about her. Jealous... who me?? I don't care if she does have a PHD. I'll never call her doctor.

The Living Zombie

When he reversed to the
genesis of his awareness,
He saw a young man full of
vitality and innovating thoughts.
Recapturing those moments,
When the world as he
understood it,
Reached out its hand,
And said, come drink of this cup
This is the promised land where
you can
dream and fulfill your most
secret desires.
It all seemed so easy until he

began the journey.
Who would have thought
The hurdles to be cleared,
The rivers to cross,
And the mountains to climb
Would appear in the form.
Of his own issue and his friends,
Whose opinions he valued so dearly.
He set out to conform, to be liked to fit it.
One day he realized he had accomplished his goal to this end.
The old spark that had set him

apart could only be fanned
to a partial flame;
Because his redundant
compromising ways would
surface to smother the flames;
and finally the spark.
He died a slow death;
Entombed in his body, a living
Zombie; a death he lived daily.

GangBusters

Bang.. Bang.. Bang...
A loud incognito
Knock.. Knock.. Knock...

Open the door before they
break it down.
The prisoners are free.

Energetic like a chained dog,
just broke loose
Through the peephole images
of three jubilant, hyper-
mischievous
Smiling faces come into view.

Their expressions asking the question
Why won't you open this door?

Hi Aunt Carol! ..We're here.
Lord, give me strength.

———————

At a Glance

This sea of tile with its
ingrained likeness to the desert
and covering, caressing every
nook and cranny
Of this incessant tread upon
span.
In some forgotten place,
The cry tim-be-r was heard.
The dreamers fashioned their
thoughts upon the pulp.
Now people stream the
corridors,
Void of any thought to the
etymology of the creative form.

The commemorative designs,
Steeped in historic valve
command attention to an eye
pleasing consistency.
The bold magnetic lights,
Placed upon the shopper's bait
Beckon each one to come.
Feast your eyes, you won't
spring the trap.
The harmony of musical sounds
in concert with the diverse
blending colors fill of the mind
with a serene ecstasy witnessed
by the older crowd sitting
dignified...

On wrought benches
Discussing the yesteryears
Without warning an invasion commences
Our aspirations for tomorrow have landed
A new surge of energy in this sheltered shoppers paradise.
From an observational view point
One gets the feeling that they,
The younger generation,
Possess an inherent understanding
that this way of life is their inheritance.

Water gushes out through the portals
In the floor like mini geysers,
Springing up while the golden glow absorbs each strand of water
An oasis in the middle of the sea of tile.
Surrounded by green leafed plants.
Pitched pennies lie inert within the pool
A tribute from our wishful thinkers.

Despairing Posterity

Dispirited thoughts crowd my mind
While pondering:
The glistening sun that tints fresh water streams;
That carved an inevitable path through the wooded place;
Are now polluted with man made contaminants.
In divers places bewildered trees
Lean against the awesome strength of the hurricane;
Or uproot as the merciless

tornado continues on its path of destruction;
Now, more fierce than every before.
The ozone layer is constantly thinning and losing the battle to shield the earth from the cancerous rays of the sun.
Man's greed is bringing about the extinction of many animals, birds, trees, the shark.
Manmade imbalance in nature
Causing chaos throughout this earth.
Genocide, that feared word among any race of people is

prevalent in the black African experience today.
The lack of self esteem-a low-self-image
Striving against a colorless society that looks upon color with distain --
Especially blacks.
This stigma is enhanced by a supposed white superiority that fosters the nation that races of color are inferior.
This misconception inevitably brings about repercussions.
Every man wants to be free from physical, mental and

religious oppression.
Sodom and Gomorrah
syndrome seems to be the order
of the day and those ahead.
There is spiritual wickedness in
high places.
People will not endure sound
doctrine. If respect became a
bottle of whiskey and humility
was a bottle of beer -- Johnny
Walker Red
would be the living dead.
Whiskey and beer would be
outcasts
And the brewery would put a
lock on its door.

The partakers would dwindle down to a precious few.

If crack made you love your neighbor as yourself or pray for them that despitefully use you— Crack heads could hardly be persuaded to try it, much less buy it.

If fornication and adultery was honorable the partakers would abhor it like the plague. Disobedience to God's natural and spiritual laws are surely leading man to his own extinction.

May the Best Man Win

I once knew two men
One stood accused by the other
When the accused found out
They refrained from facing each other
But began to low rate each other;
That low down dirty rat
There is no lower than his kind
Said the accusers.
Thus each one declared the other to be low life.

And the same tactics were employed
By both, while attempting to hurt one another.
Blinded by the animal instinct to
Retaliate, neither could see that
No one was better than the other.
Two of a kind - that unmovable will
Of the same opinion still.
Will the best man please step forward—
Alas... there was no one to answer the call.

No More Biscuits
(The death of my mother-in-law)

Looking deep into her dark brown eyes,
I took a voyage (split second) through space, I cautiously navigated through her gentle manner
And was caught in the gravitational pull of her unconditional love.
It was here I remained in orbit, she had made, me alone, a pan of biscuits, her warmth, her love, cloned itself in those tasty biscuits.

One bite exposed the inner beauty of this extraordinary woman.

In the midst of pondering my dilemma (what could I give back?)

She sent me twelve biscuits more,

My inner being cried out...

She loves me! ...she loves me!

One bright sun filled day after the

Summer had claimed its grand début

The birds were whistling their joyous strains,

The bees gathered nectar from the new born blooms, the rain had come and stayed too long.
Her eyes closed, her voice was stilled
Her hands could no longer fashion,
But everything was alright
Grief stricken at the loss
But yet I thought,
...no more biscuits.

Two Peas In a Pod
(who won)

Two women, an inevitable confrontation about to ensue. After what seems like an eternity of silence.
Their overall contempt for each other is evidenced by the eye to eye contact.
First woman speaks, "I have never in my entire life known anyone as jealous, unjust, selfish, unforgiving and as spiteful as you are."

The second woman replied, "that's exactly what I think of you"
Then both women began physically abusing each other.
If one of them had a forgiving nature there might have been no fight,
Peace is the stronger motivation not to fight.
This battle is fueled by satanic forces,
They both lost, because they are lost.

The Sower Shall Reap

Two doves sitting on the limb of
a grand old oak.
The first dove said, "You know
that young blue jay
Nesting in the hollow of that
great elm,
We use to live in the same tree.
Recently he flew away and took
some of my worms with him;
that's what I call stealing".
The second dove asked, "did
you see him take them?"
"No" answered the first dove,
"but when he departed,

I believe he worms left with him."

"Maybe the worms crawled away while you were collecting more food" argued the second dove.

The first dove snapped back... "no he stole my worms.

The second dove looked at the first dove with a puzzled expression and said, "Didn't I see you the other day flying away from the robin's nest, in the cedar in the meadow.

You were carrying worms with your feet, as well as, with your mouth. That's not stealing??"

The first dove looked indignant, quickly replying, "God forbid, I shall do such a thing." he reasoned, "the worms crawled out of the nest, therefore, the worms would not be there when the robins returned; so I figured it was better for someone to eat them, than for them to get away altogether. That's not stealing, that's using common sense.
With a heavy heart, the second dove shouted these words as she flew out of sight.
"Whatsoever a man soweth, that shall he also reap."   xxx

Subtle Parsimony

Thank you so much,
> Sister Lyn.

My mom and I enjoyed the book
She did not want the book for free.
She is willing to pay for it,
Do you want her to pay you?

Lest We Forget

Someone rejoiced
It's a boy... it's a girl
Tears of sorrow should have
run down
Like mighty Niagara Falls.
Hell on earth raged like the pit
of fire and brimstone.
A plague of terror spread
Throughout the world.
The anti Christ will show
No mercy when he reigned;
The cupboards are bare,
Soup lines are long.
Snow falls are fierce and
abundant

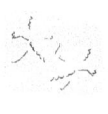 Covering the land like
an Antarctic bear.
Heat is scarce,
Winters are cold,
Laughter is diminished,
By the spilling of blood,
As one nation under God.
The eagle sought the higher
power.
After the plea was answered,
And the sun shine was no
longer dim.
Before the scab could claim
healing The nation pursued its
unthankful ways with diligence.
But for a thousand years the
called out ones,

Shall rejoice in the New Birth.
But the weeping of mortals,
Shall appear through this journey.
Heaven and earth shall pass away,
As we know it, but his word shall stand.

This Thing Called Love

They say that true love is hard to find,
That true love mellows with the passing of time.
It ferments and get better like an aged old wine,
They say that true love is not always easy to define.
But when you find it you know,
It's a breed of a different kind.
And many have declared true love is blind,
Because there is little or no desire to stray out of line.

Know this to be a true sign
When it manifests such peace
of mind;
When the road is rocky. Listen:
Don't fret, don't faint;
True love will stand the test;
Its patient its kind, its repentant;
It can be harsh cruel and
sometimes unrelenting.
After all have been said and
done,
And its quite apparent to
everyone;
The balance of passion has
tipped the scale.

Leaving one in love's tenacious grip.
Love will blossom to its fullest bloom
Then the musical organ can announce
Here comes the bride and groom.

FOOLISH PRIDE

Starting out in business
With his brand new bride,
Young, black and full of pride.

He cleaned a large gray house,
With an oversized foyer
Whose owner was a wealthy
lawyer.

One day out of need,
His budget stretched to the hilt
for sure
He ducked inside a little thrift
store.

He pondered his actions
before going in,
While he cautiously looked
around
Until anyone that knew him
Could no where be found.

But oh' what a surprise
As he stepped inside the door,
He saw the wealthy lawyer
The one he was working for
Buying every stick of furniture
setting on the floor.

He learned a lesson that day
The lives with him yet.

He threw away his foolish pride
That kept him deep in debt.

Abode Rodent

Quiet!
Dragging, scratching, gnawing
In the wall, in the loft.
We dare not speculate on what
It is hoped, not to be.

Then silence, merely a prelude
Scratch... scratch...   scratch
Throw the shoe at the ceiling
Hesitation...a squeak...scurrying

Silence...   silence approaching
sleep
Scratch... scratch...   scratch

The aggravating, horrifying truth
Repulsion, nuisance, the baby

A plan of attack, fumigate
The trap, peanut butter, cheese poison
A mouse is in the house.

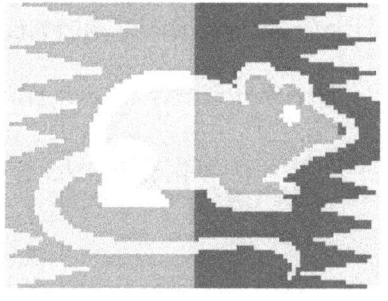

Party Chit Chat

Hi, ...hello,... How are you?
Glad to see you.
Hmmm,... quite a few people are already here. The records sound good and the food smells better!
Can we have prayer?... then everyone go to the kitchen and serve yourself.
You're not gonna eat?!!!
Yes! Right on brother... why didn't you fix my plate.
Sorry about that,... every man for himself.

Remember sisters, you're on a diet.

There's rolls..., nobody is touching the rolls.

Corn beef... huh!!!... no brisket of beef?!?!!

Can I serve someone some punch?

Nobody saying anything.

Whew! I'm tired. I worked from 6:30 this morning. Huh! Huh! Huh!

Never heard of young people so tired. Hey you all, come on up!

Honey you eat so much you can't breathe. Hi everyone, am I late?
Hey, are you leaving?
No, but I won't stay too-o-o late.
Got to get up in the morning.
Wow! Ain't much room to get by.
Plenty room, plenty room.
Western union called! Good morning, its quarter to five.
Get me some ice.
Now I'll throw my cup away.
Really, I didn't think my heart can take it. I'm afraid of heights period.

Sue said, the priest got up and started praying on the plane. Ha! Ha1! Ha! Sue said, Oh Lord this is it. I'm gonna go down stairs and go to bed.
What?!?!! She got long stringy hair and her eyes all popped out like they're swollen.
Homely, hom-e-l-y ain't the word. Then she got pregnant. She really looked bad. She walked down there just barely makin it.
Hi, thought you was suppose to be working?
There's one girl in the lab,

every time I see her, she's pregnant.
What's wrong with her?
Don't let Granma know you were there tonight.
She wanted to come, ...aw, ...aw.
Oh my little peewee; yes, she's forever with fingers in her mouth.. A little peanut.
Oh no! I know better! At this point it sounds like a barn yard full of clucking hens.
It's awful quiet back here in the kitchen. You all cut the cake?
That's a wedding ain't it??
Whose wedding, ..your's or hers? ...

How's the newly weds doing?!!
Smacks... smack ...smack... chew that gum!
Sonny, I'm trying to make it. I done made it, and I'm ready for more.
Hail! Hail! ...the gangs all here.
Bye, ...pray for me tomorrow darlin.
Goodnight.
Buzz ...Buzz ...hey ask the brother will he let us out?
All I have to say is ha.. Ha.. Ha..
We rolled with laughter.
In those days we thought

we looked good *(record: I was glad when they said unto me, let us go into the house of the Lord)*

Ring... ring... ring... Ethel, oh Ethel, don't beat around the bush. Get to the point, please! You talkin bout sleepin; she does sleep.

Do I honey... yes-ss-s baby. With all this chitter chatter, how can that brother sleep??

There's something on the record but I can't tell what it is. I want you to know its pass my bedtime.

(record: I want the world to be a better place to live). Now hear this, hear this...

Our next outing would be to Rye Beach. I went to the Museum of Natural History. I went yesterday.
What wrong with you girls, you don't go anywhere.
(record: All you need is God on your side).
Roses are red, violets are blue; sugar is sweet and so are you. Milk is milk and cream is cream; the way I love you would make a dead man dream.

(record: *You don't know whether I'm right or wrong*).
Southerners like fat women.
If you're skinny they think you're sick.
Poor, poor thing.
(record: *Everyman wants to be free*).

Mama, if I have to go to the store with all these black kids... it's rough going to the movies and taking your little brother or sister.
(record: *Quit your wicked ways*).

Aw shucks! You shouldn't have done it. Its pass your bedtime ain't it??
(record: Praise Him).

Don't wait until I get married again.. I hope I can stand the shock.
Bro. Borum's awfully quiet tonight..
He's writing... I'm ready when anybody else is.

The end

About the Author

"*Writings from Life's Treasure Chest*" is William's third book of poetry, prose, and short stories. William, known by his friends as 'Zeke' retains treasured memoirs of his many real life experiences. Words, like particles of dust waiting to be recognized, chosen and disposed. The creator through the poet, shapes the body until it is completely formed. The poem like God's instruments, comes to life. Some with greater anointing than others, when verbally expressed through the author. The personality, the emotional mood that is present at birth, is cloned to maintain the inherent quality to bring it recognition.

www.ingramcontent.com/pod-product-compliance
Lightning Source LLC
Chambersburg PA
CBHW071501070426
42452CB00041B/2053